# TAPESTRY WEAVING

## JESS BROOKE

RIGBY LIMITED · ADELAIDE
National Library of Australia Card
Number & ISBN 0 85179 730 X

ROBERT HALE & COMPANY · LONDON
ISBN 0 7091 4708 2

First published 1975
Copyright © 1975 Jessie Brooke
All rights reserved

Printed in Hong Kong

# CONTENTS

*Cover photograph "Swiss Autumn."*

*Unless otherwise stated, all articles shown in the colour plates are the work of the author.*
*Photography by D. A. Brooke.*

# WHAT IS TAPESTRY?

Tapestry is sometimes referred to as "picture weaving." The fact that it often uses short ends of yarn suggests that it was the earliest form of weaving, as the materials used for weaving centuries ago would only have been available in short lengths. Weaving began long before the advent of even the simplest looms as we know them.

Tapestry weaving is a type of 2-shaft weaving. It is a simple weave with unlimited possibilities. No other technique offers the weaver so much freedom in the use of colour. The work proceeds slowly, often at the rate of only 1 inch per hour on a 30-inch width, but it is enjoyable and rewarding.

Weavers of modern tapestries employ techniques which have been used by various peoples for thousands of years. Traditional techniques are combined in unusual ways and weavers experiment freely with new ideas. A woven tapestry can be a replica of a painting, but it should have a *specifically woven* character. Mona Hessing of Sydney is one of the many weavers whose work has a specifically woven character.

## A DEFINITION OF TAPESTRY

The term "tapestry" is used in two senses. First, it refers broadly to any heavy woven material, even one which has been embroidered. One hundred years ago, the meaning was narrowed to refer specifically to a weave in which the weft threads were packed so tightly that the warp yarns were concealed altogether, giving a solid weft-faced surface. This implies that many so-called modern tapestries are not tapestries at all; nor is the Bayeux tapestry a true tapestry. In a true tapestry, front and back are identical except for any loose ends which, if not turned in, will hang loose on the wrong side. The weft threads are woven in where their colour appears in the design, so forming the pattern and completely covering the warp.

The actual method of weaving differs from one country to another. In European tapestry, a slit is left where wefts of one colour meet with wefts of another colour. Wefts of different colours interlock in Oriental tapestry, while in many primitive tapestries weft threads of one colour are dovetailed with threads of another colour.

## COPTIC WEAVING

The earliest examples of tapestry weaving to survive were found in the tomb of an Egyptian king and have been dated about 1400 B.C. The work of Coptic weavers has also survived from the 2nd century A.D. The Copts (Christian descendants of the ancient Egyptians) departed from the style of weaving introduced by the Greeks and developed their own weaving style. This included the practice of weaving from the side if appropriate to the design, and allowing the weft to follow a curved line to emphasise the design.

## FRENCH GOBELINS

In the 17th century, Flemish weavers in Paris acquired the premises of the Gobelin family who had been cloth dyers. In 1667, the first Gobelin manufactory became the Royal Factory. The name "Gobelin" later became almost synonymous with tapestry. Gobelins were woven on the *haute lisse* (high warp) looms, with vertical warps. Elsewhere in France, at Aubusson and Beauvais, weavers worked on *basse lisse* (low warp) looms, with horizontal warps.

Modern French tapestries are woven in vast workrooms by skilled craftsmen who serve an apprenticeship of five years before they gain a certificate of competency.

## NAVAHO WEAVING

The Navaho "serape" is a beautiful example of tapestry weaving. It is 3 or 4 feet wide and 6 or 7 feet long; folded lengthwise and worn over the shoulder, it can be used as an overcoat, a raincoat, a cushion for sitting or kneeling, and as a blanket for sleeping. The tapestry weaving of these American Indians, with its areas of solid colour, offers great freedom in design, and is recognisable everywhere by its clean designs made up of evenly balanced geometrical units.

## TAPESTRY OR WALL HANGING?

There is now some doubt about whether to call certain woven pieces tapestries or wall hangings. If the narrower meaning of the term "tapestry" is used as a criterion, these pieces are not tapestries unless the warp is completely covered, and must be called wall hangings. But, we tend to use the term in its wider and more ancient sense, and apply it to all textiles which are intended as wall decorations. Then the terms "tapestry" and "wall hanging" are virtually synonymous.

# EQUIPMENT AND YARNS

## THE LOOM

Tapestry can be woven on any loom which is suitable for 2-shaft weaving. It can be a 2-shaft loom, a 4-shaft loom, or even a 16-shaft loom. It can be woven just as easily on a rug loom, or on a simple frame; even a picture frame or an old bedstead can be used. It is important, though, that the loom or frame should be solidly built as there is considerable strain, or tension, on the warp threads.

## WARP YARNS

The warp yarn should be smooth and strong. Linen is lustrous, long-lasting, and has great strength. Cotton is best for the beginner as its softness makes it easier to handle.

A suitable warp can be made from 10/12s cotton or, if preferred, 3/9s linen.

## WEFT YARNS

It is recommended that beginners use 2-ply carpet yarn for the weft. It is readily available and can sometimes be purchased from a carpet factory at a low price. If available only in large quantities, it can be shared by a number of weavers.

With a finer weft yarn use a finer warp. Your own experience will guide you.

## BOBBINS

Bobbins are sometimes used to hold the weft yarns. They may be of the Gobelin or Aubusson type (see Figure 1).

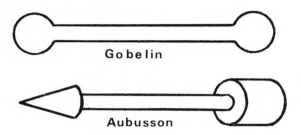

Go be lin

Aubusson

*Figure 1*

A simpler way of keeping the wefts in order is to wind them into "dollies" or "butterflies." A foolproof system for winding dollies is described on page 16.

## COMB

An animal's comb with metal teeth (eight or ten to the inch) and a wooden handle can be used as a beater for combing the wefts into place (see Figure 2).

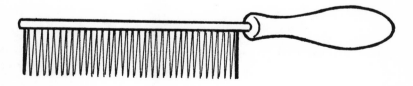

*Figure 2*

## SHEARS

Instead of scissors, shears can be used (see Figure 3). They are not an essential piece of equipment,

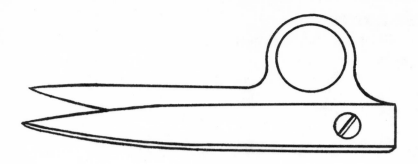

*Figure 3*

but are very useful for trimming ends close to the surface of the work.

## WOOL NEEDLE

The weft is usually laid in with the fingers, but sometimes a wool needle is useful for dealing with awkward weft ends—for example, when a new colour is introduced at the selvedge of the tapestry.

An area of "wrapping" (see page 42) sometimes results in a weft end which cannot be neatly woven in. In this case, the weft end should be threaded into a wool needle and taken down into the work along a warp end. Bring the needle up after an inch and, with shears or scissors, trim the yarn close to the surface of the work.

# WARPING THE FRAME

A simple frame of the type shown in Figure 4 is ideal for tapestry weaving and is easily moved about. It can be used to make small wall-hangings, cushions, shoulder bags, table runners, and even a large tapestry or a rug if these are woven in sections.

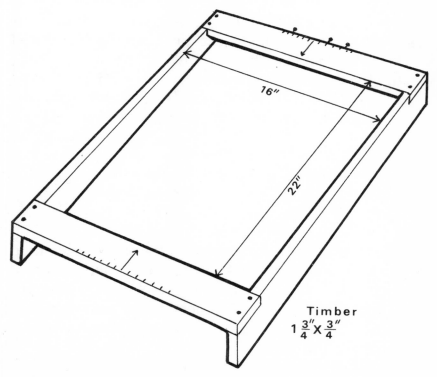

Timber
$1\frac{3}{4}''\times\frac{3}{4}''$

16"

22"

*Figure 4*

There is no need for a spacing system using nails or grooves. The ends of the frame, top and bottom, are marked off in inches from the centre. When you have decided on the width of the piece to be woven, fix small tacks or drawing pins securely in the top of the frame at the appropriate marks, to the right and left of the centre.

## ESTIMATING WARP QUANTITIES

It is quite simple to estimate the amount of warp yarn required, and any yarn supplier should be able to tell you how many yards there are in each pound of yarn.

10/12s cotton has 40 yards to each ounce. A warp which is 6 inches wide on a simple frame will use a good deal less than 1 ounce of yarn.

$$\text{Number of warp ends in 6-in. warp} = 36$$
$$\text{Each warp end} = 24 \text{ in. (or } \tfrac{2}{3}\text{ yd.)}$$
$$\therefore \text{ Length of warp yarn required} = 36 \times \tfrac{2}{3} \text{ yd.}$$
$$= 24 \text{ yd.}$$

$$40 \text{ yd. of 10/12s cotton} = 1 \text{ oz.}$$
$$\therefore 24 \text{ yd.} = \tfrac{1}{40} \times 24 \text{ oz.}$$
$$= \cdot 6 \text{ oz.}$$

In other words, a 6-inch warp on the frame described will use ·6 ounce of 10/12s cotton. It follows that a 12-inch warp on a 24-inch frame will use 1·2 ounces, a 12-inch warp on a 48-inch frame will use 2·4 ounces, a 24-inch warp on a 48-inch frame will use 4·8 ounces, and so on.

It is wise to over-estimate your requirements and so avoid the inconvenience of running out of yarn.

## THE WARPING

Stand the frame on its bottom left-hand corner, remembering that the tacks are at the top. Rest the corner of the frame on the table, or on another chair if you are seated. Make a loop about 4 inches from the end of the warping yarn. Loop it over the left-hand tack at the top of the frame. Wind the yarn *clockwise* around the frame three times for each inch of the required width, and *one extra time*. Keep a very firm tension as you wind. Each successive round can be held firmly in place with the thumb and fingers of the left hand as the winding proceeds.

When winding the last round, take the yarn behind the right-hand tack at the top of the frame, once around the tack, and back to the starting point, so that the two ends can be securely tied. Tie them with a slip knot and draw them as tight as possible. Then make a reef knot.

## WARP TENSION

The warp should be very taut, as the tapestry must be worked on a firm foundation. Uneven tension results in uneven work, and can cause "bubbling." Slack tension in the outer warp ends will result in uneven edges. There is very little, if any, take-up in tapestry weaving. A cotton warp is more likely than a linen warp to stretch and slacken as you weave.

## THE SHED STICK

This should measure 18 inches so that it rests on the sides of the frame when in position. It should be 1 inch wide and about $\frac{3}{16}$ inch thick. When the warp is in position, insert the shed stick so that the top threads are pushed *down* and the bottom threads are lifted *up*. Position the shed stick near the top of the frame.

## TWINING THE WARP

Twining ensures even spacing of the warp ends. Take a length of strong cotton or linen yarn four times the width of the frame and fold it in half. Attach it to the left side of the frame quite near the bottom (see Figure 5). Tie an overhand knot at the left of the first warp end (see Figure 6).

*Figure 5*

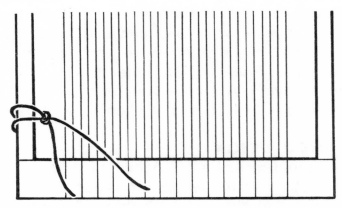

*Figure 6*

Twining takes up every warp end. Stand the shed stick on its side and carry one of the twining threads through the shed to the right-hand side of the warp. As a temporary measure, fasten it securely to the right-hand side of the frame.

To insert the second twining thread into the second shed, pass it over the warp where the first thread goes under the warp. Each time the second thread goes *under* a warp end, it also goes *under* the first thread (see Figure 7). The action is *over*, *under*, and

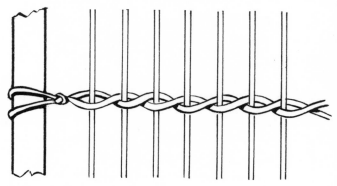

*Figure 7*

*down*. As you work, tighten the twining threads and check that there are six warp ends evenly spaced between each inch mark.

When every warp end has been bound, make another overhand knot to the right of the last warp end, to correspond with the one on the left. Fasten the two ends to the right side of the frame to correspond with the fastening on the left.

Although the beginner may find the twining operation laborious, it quickly becomes automatic. It can be repeated at the other end of the warp, but this is not strictly necessary. If you are working on a large frame, a second twining in the middle helps to maintain spacing and prevent narrowing of the warp. The second pair of twining threads can be pushed up with the comb as work proceeds.

## CONTINUOUS WARP

Your finished work will measure about 14 inches by 18 inches if you use the full width and length of your frame. As you work nearer to the top of the frame it will become difficult to make a shed large enough to lay in the weft. It is possible, however, to weave a piece at least twice as long if you weave on a continuous warp.

Firstly, using tape, secure a rod $\frac{1}{2}$ inch to $\frac{3}{4}$ inch in diameter to the top of the frame (see Figure 8).

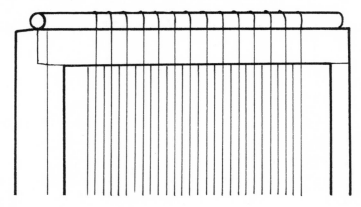

*Figure 8*

Wind the warp *six* times around the frame for each inch of the width you have decided on for your finished work. Insert the shed stick in the top layer of warp ends only, passing it under one and over the

14

next across the warp. Twine only the top layer of threads and weave on this layer. As work proceeds you will need to move the warp on. Bring the top rod forward. Roll it down the wood at the top of the frame and put it aside. Cut the twining threads so that they are no longer attached to the sides of the frame. Press down on your shed stick and ease the work down so that it moves around the frame, until the last weft is at a convenient working level. Insert the rod between the two layers again. Move it up to the top of the frame and roll it up between the warp and the wood until it is back in its original position.

## CORRECTING WARP TENSION

If the warp "softens" and loses tension, insert a rod between the top of the frame and the warp, as described above. The diameter of the rod will be determined by the amount of slack which needs to be taken up.

# THE WEAVING

## WINDING A DOLLY

Take a weft thread about 2 yards long. With the right hand, take the end of the yarn three times clockwise around the left thumb, then forward, and around the little finger (see Figure 9). Continue winding in a

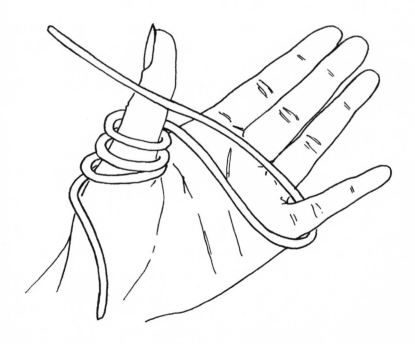

*Figure 9*

figure of eight around the thumb and the little finger. Finally, take the yarn forward around the thumb, and tie two or three half-hitches firmly around the centre of the dolly (see Figure 10). Use the yarn from

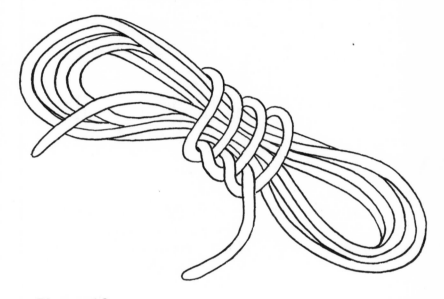

*Figure 10*

the thumb end—it will pull out easily as you work. If you start the half-hitches at the *thumb* end there will be *no knots* at the end of the yarn.

## LAYING IN THE WEFT

Remember that this is a plain weave and you will be working in two tabby sheds. The shed obtained when you stand the shed stick on its side is called the *upper* shed. The opposite shed, which is picked up with the fingers, is called the *lower* shed.

Starting at the right side, lay in enough weft in

17

the *lower* shed to cover no more than 2 inches of
warp. Leave this weft in a slight arc (see Figure 11)

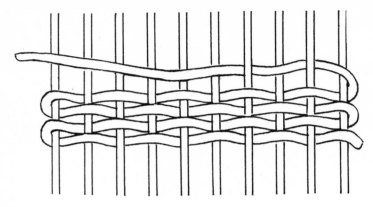

*Figure 11*

before beating it into position with the comb. This
slight slack in the weft allows it to go under and over
the taut warp (see Figure 12), covering it completely

*Figure 12*

as the work proceeds, and packing down well without causing any "drawing in," or narrowing, of the
work. This is the *first pick*.

Take the weft around the last warp end, open the
*upper* shed by turning the shed stick on its side, and
lay in your second line of weft from the left, again

working over only 1 or 2 inches of warp at a time. This is the *second pick. Two picks* make *one pass.*

## WEFT TENSION

Too much tension in the weft causes a narrowing of the work. Remember that the weft goes *down under* one warp and *up over* the next (see Figure 12). Check the width of your work with a ruler every inch or so to ensure that it is not losing width. As you become more experienced you will not need to check it as often.

Beating the weft hard results in a greater number of picks to the inch. It produces a hard textile, suitable for a rug, but not so attractive for a tapestry which will hang on the wall. The weft must cover the warp, but should not be too tightly compacted. Using 2-ply carpet yarn for the weft on a warp of 10/12s cotton set at 6 ends per inch, the number of picks per inch is about thirty.

## RHYTHM 292 171 / 746 · 14

If you work methodically and without haste, you will develop a natural rhythm of your own and you will be able to work faster. Weave in plain colour across the width of your warp for about an inch for practice in developing your own rhythm.

## ENDS

At the beginning of your work leave a "tail" of yarn about $1\frac{1}{2}$ inches long when you weave your first pick. Weave in the tail when you are weaving your second pick, and push the last $\frac{1}{2}$ inch or so through to the underside of your work.

Similarly, when the weft runs out pick up a new weft thread and weave straight on, tucking the two ends, each $\frac{3}{4}$ inch to 1 inch long, through to the back of the work.

Traditionally, these ends were left on the surface of the work as weaving progressed, and so the weaver was working from the back, or the wrong side, of the tapestry. Where it is intended to add loops, tufts, or other surface decoration, the ends can be pushed through to the back so that the weaver has the right side of his work facing him.

Where it is necessary to introduce a new colour at the edge of the work, the tail can be woven back in the next pick, as at the beginning, or it can be threaded into a wool needle and taken *down* into the work (or *up*, later) along the last warp end, and trimmed neatly with shears or scissors.

## ESTIMATING WEFT QUANTITIES

One pound of 2-ply carpet yarn is more than enough for a tapestry measuring 20 inches square (400 square inches). Again, it is best to over-estimate the amount of yarn needed, to avoid inconvenience. To estimate quantities of different colours, draw the design on squared paper and count the squares of colour.

Let each square represent 1 square inch. In a given design there may be the following colours:

| | | |
|---|---|---|
| Purple | 200 sq. require 8 oz. 2-ply carpet yarn. |
| Red | 100 sq. require 4 oz. 2-ply carpet yarn. |
| Orange | 100 sq. require 4 oz. 2-ply carpet yarn. |
| Total | 400 sq. require 1 lb. 2-ply carpet yarn. |

Remembering that work measuring 400 square inches needs 16 ounces of weft yarn, it is a simple matter to work out quantities of each colour. Even when dealing with many colours in small quantities, you will soon be able to estimate your requirements.

# DESIGN AND THE CARTOON

In modern tapestry weaving there is wonderful scope for experimenting with colour, design, and texture. Begin by weaving a small piece or sample, working in a design as you weave. Using a selection of yarns of attractive and related colours, choose a dominant colour, and arrange the others to balance over the surface of your tapestry. To develop skill in design you need to experiment with it. Communicate your ideas to others through your choice of colour and texture, but at the same time remember that *simplicity in design* is important.

There are designs all around you in many different forms. They appear in common objects with flowing or neat, uncluttered lines; in objects of nature—a flower or tree, a fruit or vegetable, which, when sliced, reveals a marvellous structure; in photographs and paintings; in advertisements in newspapers. There are endless sources of inspiration for tapestry design.

Without directly copying the work of another artist, which is an unrewarding exercise as well as denying your own talent for imagination expression, you may derive from it an initial idea or starting point from which your own ideas can develop. You may find that while you are working on one piece of weaving, other designs will suggest themselves to you. It is only a matter of making a start, and then the biggest problem is having enough time to carry out all your ideas.

Experiment with colour combinations by using the many techniques available to obtain different effects. If you have a definite design in mind, or if you are planning a fairly large piece of work, you would be wise to use a cartoon.

## CARTOONS

The cartoon is a full-size outline of the design for a tapestry. Architects' tracing paper is ideal for the purpose; white kitchen paper, butchers' paper, or grease-proof paper serve reasonably well but tear easily and need careful handling. If the cartoon is to be large, or in use for a long time and subjected to much handling, architects' tracing paper is the best paper to use.

The piece of paper should be large enough to be attached with masking tape to the frame, behind the warp. If you are working on a loom you can pin your cartoon to the beginning of your work, behind the warp, and it can be rolled on with the weaving as you proceed.

## DRAWING THE DESIGN

A small sketch of your design can be easily blown up to size by the technique of "enlarging by squares." Square your small sketch by dividing it into equal squares with a pencil and ruler, or by tracing it on to transparent squared paper (see Figure 13). Then re-draw it on to paper which is the size you wish your completed tapestry to be, and is divided into squares

*Figure 13*

equal in number to the squares in the original. Draw your design, one square at a time, until you have completed the enlarged copy of the original.

Make the cartoon as detailed as you wish. You may prefer to work out the details as you weave, using only the main lines of the design in your cartoon as a guide. All sorts of ideas will form as you work, and as you become familiar with the techniques at your command. Larger tapestries may need to be planned in greater detail so that you can determine approximate yarn and colour requirements.

# COLOURS AND TAPESTRY TECHNIQUES

## SIMPLE COLOUR EFFECTS

Having woven 1 inch in plain colour, vary the weft colours successively and assess the effects, looking for discordant and harmonious colour combinations. Try plying two single yarns of different colours, and weaving with the resulting yarn. Ply with fine lurex for a sparkling effect.

## HORIZONTAL COLOUR CHANGES

For special effects vary the colour of your picks in a regular scheme. A single pick in a contrasting colour gives a row of dots (see Figure 14).

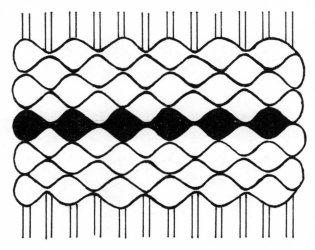

*Figure 14*

## VERTICAL STRIPES

Using two contrasting colours in alternate picks makes vertical stripes (see Figure 15).

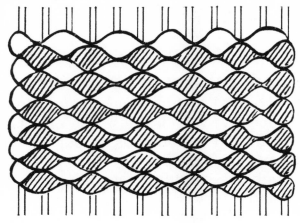

*Figure 15*

## HORIZONTAL STRIPES

Alternate *passes* in two contrasting colours make horizontal stripes (see Figure 16).

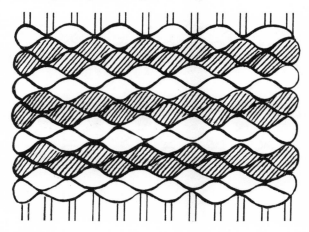

*Figure 16*

## VERTICAL COLOUR CHANGES

Having reached a point in your weaving when one colour does not carry across the entire width of the warp, you may want to introduce a second colour.

Lay in the first colour from the *right*. Introduce the second colour from the *left*; it will be in the same shed as the first colour. The two wefts travel in *opposite* directions, and make a pair (see Figure 17).

*Figure 17*

If you follow the practice of pairing colours, you will have no problems making a colour change at a different point. It follows that if you wish to introduce a third colour between the first two, the pairs system will be upset (see Figure 18). To avoid this, introduce

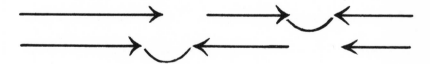

*Figure 18*

two wefts of the new colour (see Figure 19). If you have two new colours to introduce, the pairs system will not be upset, as long as you ensure that the two new wefts are travelling in the right directions.

*Figure 19*

## SLITS

The *kilim* (or khelim) technique is the simplest way of dealing with adjacent areas of colour. A slit is left in the work wherever there is a vertical colour change. The technique lends itself to designs which are made up of geometric units, in which the design lines proceed by steps (see Figures 20 and 21). To

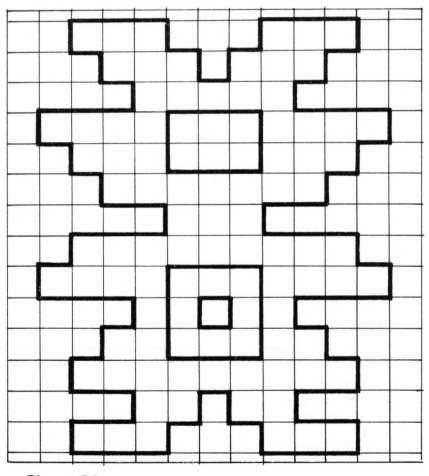

*Figure 20*

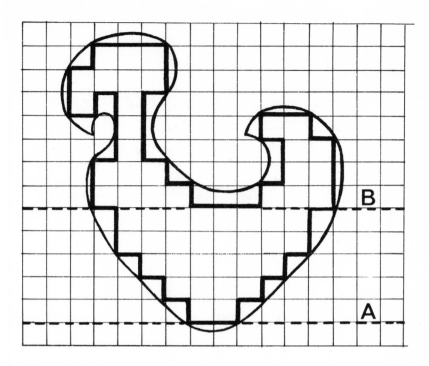

*Figure 21*

make a vertical line, there must be a vertical colour change, which results in a slit. If the vertical lines are long, the slits will be long; it is best to avoid long vertical lines in design. When this technique was used in Gothic and Renaissance tapestries, long slits were stitched together after the tapestry was completed.

Remember to use the pairs system (see above) when introducing additional wefts. Introduce the first colour from the *right*, and weave as far as the warp end which defines the limit of that colour area. Turn the weft around that warp end and work as far as the design allows on its section of the warp only.

29

Introduce the second colour from the *left* and weave it similarly (see Figure 22). The third colour is

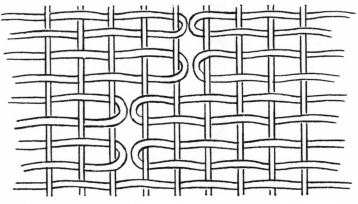

*Figure 22*

introduced from the *right*, and so on. It is much quicker to work with one colour in a small area, change colour, and work with the new colour in another small area, than to change colours continually across one weft line, working across the entire width of the warp.

You must remember, however, that if proceeding by steps you must build up your work from the bottom. You will not be able to go back and weave an area below one you have already woven.

To make a kilim design, draw the shape you want on squared paper and mark in the appropriate horizontal and vertical lines to outline the design (see Figure 21). You will notice that there are similarities between kilim design and Fair Isle knitting. Remember to avoid long vertical lines. When working the design shown in Figure 21, you will be working with three dollies at A, and five dollies at B. You will have

**Colour plate 1** *Two samplers.*

**Colour plate 2** *A first attempt at free use of tapestry techniques and colour. Woven by Jeanne Plummer.*

**Colour plate 3** *"Soft Centre."*

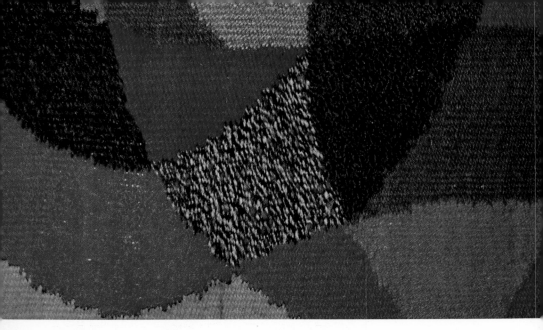

**Colour plate 4** *Detail of "Swiss Autumn" (see cover photograph).*

**Colour plate 5** *Detail of "Harvest."*

**Colour plate 6** *Detail of ''Pyalong.''*

**Colour plate 7** *Detail of "Fantail."*

**Colour plate 8** *Detail of "Jungle Bird."*

**Colour plate 9** *"Funny Face"* — *see page 51.*

introduced two new wefts and so the pairs will not be upset.

A pattern of slits in a plain colour tapestry, or even in a tone-on-tone tapestry which incorporates slits as an element of the design, can be visually very satisfying. Subtle effects of this kind can be created more successfully with light shades, as interesting shadows appear on the surface of the tapestry. In mediaeval tapestries a lacy appearance was given to the ceremonial robes of certain figures by tightening the weft to open small slits. This is illustrated by some of the tapestries in Joseph Jobé's *Art of Tapestry* (see Bibliography, page 64).

## SINGLE DOVETAILING

This is a primitive technique which ensures that there is no slit where a vertical colour change occurs. There is, however, some bulk where the wefts are doubled as they turn around the same warp end.

Introduce your second colour as before in accordance with your design, but take each weft alternately around the same warp end (see Figure 23).

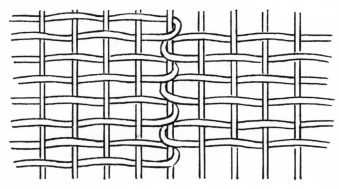

*Figure 23*

## TRIPLE DOVETAILING

This is similar to single dovetailing except that the two wefts are taken round the same warp for *three* passes each, alternately. The weaving is then a little faster as you do not have to change colour after each pass. It gives the effect of a serration (see Figure 24).

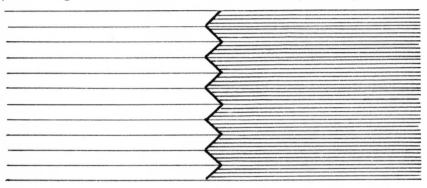

*Figure 24*

When weaving the first group of the second colour there may be some difficulty in beating, where the wefts pile up at the point of colour change. But, the resiliency of the wool ensures the adjustment of the weft line as you weave on.

In *Flemish Weaving* by Gertrud Ingers (see Bibliography, page 64) the effect of using triple dove-tailing to define rooftops is shown in the back cover illustration and in Figures 51 and 78.

## INTERLOCKING

A flatter intersection of colour is achieved with interlocking, which is the best method for smooth, neat vertical colour changes. Adjacent wefts are taken *around each other* between two warp ends (see

Figure 25). Once again the colours should be woven towards each other in pairs in the same shed, so that the colour change can be made at any point. The point of colour change can then be altered at any time without the problem of the weft being in the wrong shed.

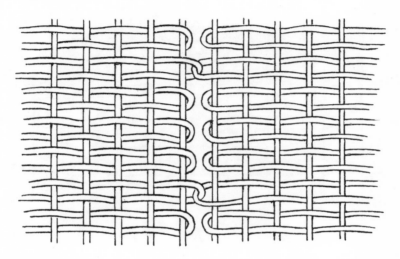

*Figure 25*

## HATCHING

Hatching, or introducing fine lines of various colours, is used to give an effect of shading or as an independent decorative device. Single irregular hatching, and two examples of triple hatching, can be seen in sampler B, shown in colour plate 1.

## CURVES

Curved lines can be obtained by interlocking adjacent weft colours along a curved line in the cartoon (see colour plate 4).

Alternatively, an area of weft can be built up in one colour and the second colour woven in a curved line, above this area (see Figure 26).

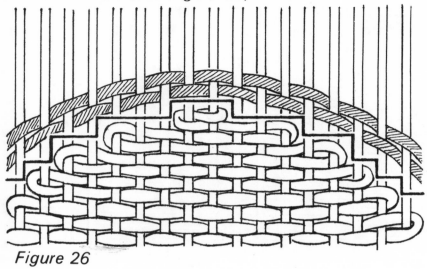

*Figure 26*

"Lozenges" can be woven if the reverse process is carried out first. An area is left *unwoven* and the weft line is taken down into it in a curved line. The inside of the curve is then filled in, and an area built up to serve as a foundation for the upper edge of the lozenge.

# SURFACE INTEREST

The use of textured yarns is the simplest way of giving surface interest to tapestry weaving. Handspun yarns, in particular, "lift" the surfaces and bring them to life. Good effects can be achieved with fancy knitting yarns, such as bouclé, loop mohair, and tweed yarns. Some fine yarns are best doubled. They may be plied on the spinning wheel, or you can simply take two ends at once when winding dollies. If the fine yarn is thick enough not to need doubling, and is used singly in conjunction with basic 2-ply carpet yarn, you may need to lay in extra picks of the finer yarn to compensate for the slight variation in thickness.

For a special effect, ply a smooth yarn loosely with a bouclé yarn. Experiment with handspinning to produce interesting yarns. *Your Handspinning* by Elsie Davenport (see Bibliography, page 63) has plenty of ideas for spinning unusual yarns.

## RYA KNOTS

The use of tufts or long strands on the surface of a wall hanging give it a third dimension. The special qualities of interesting handspun yarns are more readily appreciated if used in this way (see colour plate 8).

Lengths of yarn are pre-cut to the required length. A beautiful soft effect is given if the yarn is broken instead of cut. This is best done over scissor blades, but it is hard work, especially with carpet yarns, most of which have a 20 per cent nylon content.

A gauge for cutting the tufts can be made by folding a strong piece of cardboard of the appropriate width. Wind the yarn around the folded cardboard as many times as the number of tufts desired. Insert the tip of the scissors between the two layers of cardboard and cut (see Figure 27). You may prefer to wind

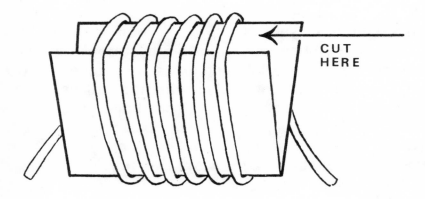

CUT HERE

*Figure 27*

the yarn around your fingers, regulating the length of the tufts by the spread of your fingers. This results in slight irregularities in the length which make the hanging more interesting.

Take the tuft in your left hand, holding it by the centre. Lay it across the pair of warps where you wish to weave it in. Bring the ends *down behind* the two warps and *up between* them (see Figure 28). Tighten the tuft by drawing on the ends, and comb it into position. Try combining yarns and colours in the tufts, with two or three ends in each, varying them as you please.

Where the tufts do not extend to the full width of the warp, lay in extra weft to compensate for the bulkiness of the tufted areas (see Figure 28). Experience will guide you in estimating how many extra passes are needed.

*Figure 28*

The rya knot, a Scandinavian technique, is identical to the Turkish or Ghiordes knot.

## PERSIAN KNOTS

These knots take up less space in the warp and this is the reason why Persian carpets have such a reputation for fineness. In fact, it is claimed that they have as many as 600 knots to the square inch.

The tuft is woven over pairs of warp ends, going under one warp end and *back* under the previous one (see Figure 29). This gives a right-handed Persian

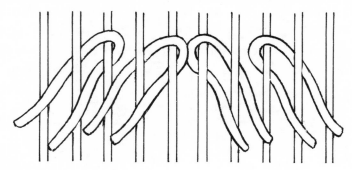

*Figure 29*

knot. It can be worked from the opposite direction to make a left-handed knot. A hanging with alternate vertical stripes of right-handed and left-handed Persian knots will have a subtle effect of light and shade.

## SPANISH KNOTS

A simpler knot, which takes up even less space in the warp, is the Spanish knot. In this the tuft is simply taken right around a single warp end (see Figure 30).

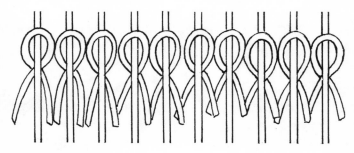

*Figure 30*

## SOUMAK

Soumak rugs, rarely woven today, are very beautiful. Soumak is a region in Iran (formerly Persia) quite near the Caucasian Sea. Soumak weaving has the appearance of embroidered chain stitch. The movement of the weft is similar to embroidered stem stitch. The soumak technique can be used for wall hangings with a double weft over four warp ends (see colour plate 6). The double weft may be of one colour or two.

Starting on the right, take the weft over four warps and back under two. Repeat the process on the next pick, from left to right. As with tufting, extra passes need to be woven alongside the soumak to compensate for its bulkiness (see Figure 31).

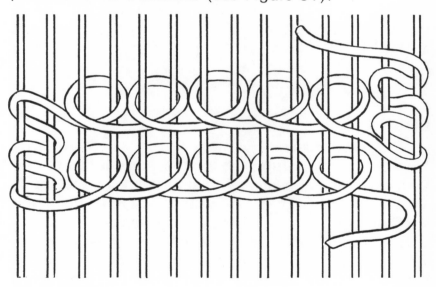

*Figure 31*

## SWEDISH KNOT

This technique, the reverse of soumak, is seldom

used, but is charming in effect, and very fine when worked with a single weft over two warp ends.

The weft goes under two warp ends and back over one. Notice the directions taken by the weft at right and left of the work (see Figure 32).

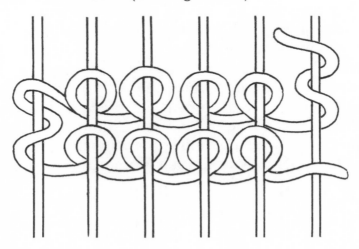

*Figure 32*

## LOOPS

Another technique which can be used by the weaver is that of lifting the weft to make loops on the surface of the tapestry. The frequency of the loops and the number of plain weave picks between the rows of loops can be varied as the weaver sees fit.

It is suggested that the loops be made with the weft travelling from right to left. Use a knitting needle or a flat stick for a gauge, which can be as thick or as thin as you wish. After weaving the loop line, do not remove the gauge until you have woven another plain pick. Beat this line of weft into position, then remove the gauge (see Figure 33).

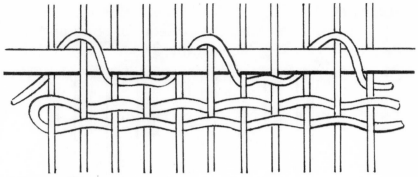

*Figure 33*

## BEADS

Beads may be used in the warp or the weft. If they are strung on the warp it is best to arrange the warp ends so that they can be untied and the beads threaded on when required, in accordance with your design (see colour plate 3). When used in the weft they can be threaded directly on to the weft if they have a large enough eye. If they are small beads with an eye too small to take the weft, thread them on strong sewing cotton, preferably of a colour which matches that of the main weft. Lay in this second thread as you weave. Make sure that the ends of this auxiliary thread are securely woven in, or they will not stay in position, particularly if the beads are heavy glass ones.

Craft shops everywhere carry good stocks of beads. Another excellent source is the opportunity shop, where one can often find necklaces which are now out of fashion but useful to the weaver who wants to add interest to a tapestry. If you have access to clay and a kiln you can make your own ceramic beads to incorporate in your weaving.

41

## WRAPPING

This technique has the effect of opening the surface of a tapestry (see Figure 34A).

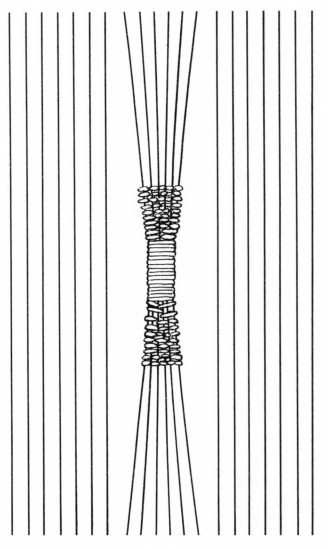

*Figure 34A*

Start with *six* warp ends. Weave two passes on these, and then treat each outside pair as one, so that you are virtually weaving on *four* ends. Weave two passes on these four ends. Then, treat each group of three as one, so that you are virtually weaving on *two* ends. Weave two passes on these two ends. Then, take the weft around all six ends, treating the six ends as *one*. Wrap the weft around this group of six ends, for as long as desired. (See Figure 34B.) The process is similar to that of decreasing in knitting.

You can vary the colour along the wrapped section by firmly holding the ends of the first and a second colour along the line of the warps, and including them in the wrapping. After four turns of the weft, trim one off close to the wrapping. After four more turns, the second end can be trimmed off. The trimming is staggered to avoid sudden loss or increase of bulk in the wrapped section (see colour plate 7).

Restore the six warp ends to their original position and sequence by reversing the decreasing process. More passes are needed now, as the warps do not spread out as easily as they draw in.

## WEAVING ORDER

When working on a particular area of the tapestry such as a wrapped section, dispose the wefts so that they are all lying in directions away from the area where you are working. In Figure 35 the areas of colour are lettered in the order in which they should be woven. A design of this kind, with no strong vertical lines, can be woven without any of the techniques of dovetailing or interlocking. The colour changes flow in smooth lines with no steep angles.

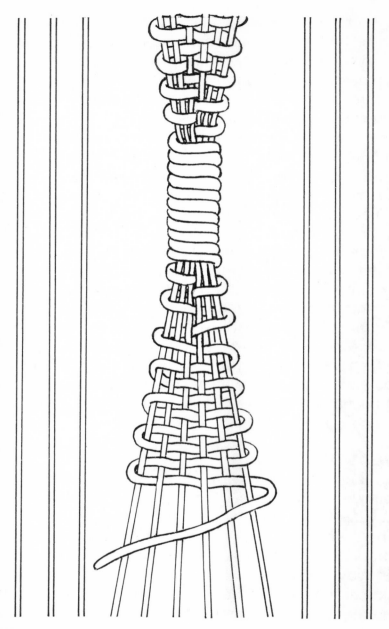

*Figure 34B*

44

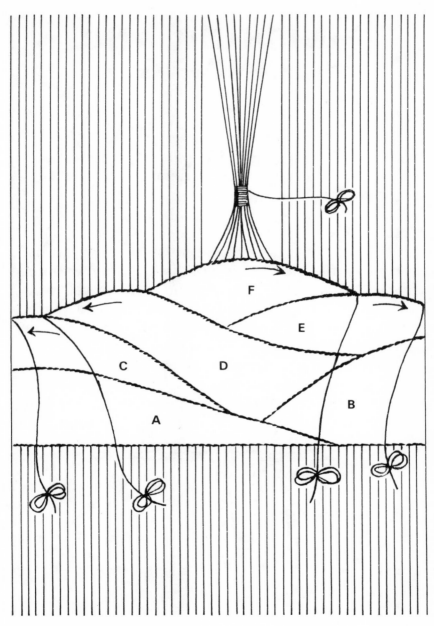

*Figure 35*

# FINISHING AND HANGING

The method of finishing and hanging a tapestry can be considered as part of the general design as soon as you begin the weaving.

## FINISHING

It is seldom necessary to iron the work. If you have overbeaten the weft, your work is more likely to need ironing. In this case, take an old bath towel, wet it completely, wring it as dry as possible, and place it between the iron and the weaving. Have the iron quite hot, but do not apply too much pressure.

The simplest finish at the bottom of a wall hanging is a fringe. The warp ends are cut in pairs, and tied with an overhand knot, which is pushed up as near as possible to the weft (see Figure 36). The warp ends

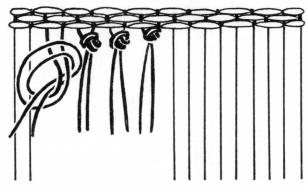

*Figure 36*

can be knotted in pairs or in groups of three or more. Macramé, crochet, or plaiting can be used to add further interest. A small wall hanging can be given extra length if a fringe of weft yarn is knotted on at the bottom. Use a crochet hook of the appropriate size to take the fringes through the work (see Figure 37 and colour plate 3).

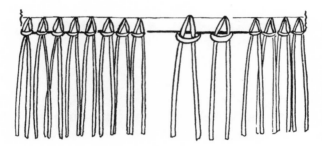

*Figure 37*

Where a tapestry has been woven from the side, the selvedges will be at the top and bottom of the work, and the side finishing will need to be done after the work leaves the loom, as side fringes are not always in keeping with a tapestry. The sides should be machine-stitched as near as possible to the first and last weft lines, to prevent unravelling. Use a zig-zag stitch if possible or, better still, stitch it with the wavy line of stitching which some machines do automatically. Machine a facing of a suitable fabric such as sail-cloth on the right side, turn it on to the reverse side of the tapestry, and stitch it invisibly by hand. Cut a strip twice the required width, fold it along the centre, and place the raw edges to the raw edge of the tapestry (see Figure 38). Alternatively,

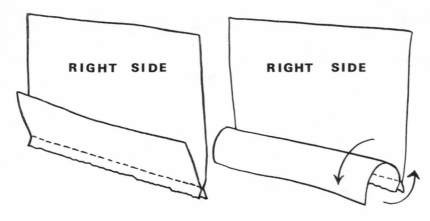

*Figure 38*

use upholsterers' webbing about $1\frac{1}{4}$ inches wide, and
not too heavy. Stitch this on top of the tapestry outside the fold line and turn it straight under (see
Figure 39). Secure it with invisible stitches. Then

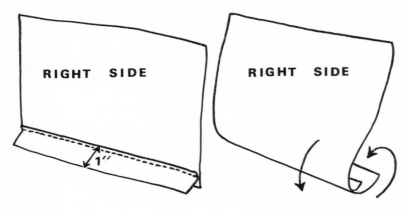

*Figure 39*

hand-stitch a casing of the same material to the back
of the tapestry $\frac{1}{6}$ inch from the top edge, allowing
enough space to insert a suitable rod or batten.

## HANGING

Narrow battens, rods, tubular metal, bamboo strips, or sticks are all suitable for hanging a wall hanging or tapestry. If pleasing to look at and in keeping with the tapestry, they can be woven in at the end, so that there is no necessity for a lot of finishing when the work comes off the loom. Insert the rod in the opposite shed to the last line of weaving. Tie the warp off, enclosing the rod with overhand knots of two, three, or four warp ends. The simplest method is to use a hollow metal rod through which a stout nylon line can be taken. If using wooden rods, or battens, attach the nylon thread with small screw eyes.

# SAMPLERS TO WEAVE

## PROJECT 1: A SAMPLER

Using two strongly contrasting colours, weave a sampler incorporating the techniques described in "Colours and Tapestry Techniques" (see page 25). These are plain colour weaving, spots, vertical stripes, horizontal stripes, slits, single dovetailing, triple dovetailing, interlocking, hatching (single, irregular, and triple), curves, and wrapping (see page 42). Suggested size—6 inches by 12 inches.

## PROJECT 2: A COLOUR SAMPLER

With a selection of your favourite colours, weave a small tapestry. At first, take the colours at random, then select them to produce a balanced arrangement of colours and shades, practising techniques used in Project 1. Suggested size—10 inches by 15 inches.

## PROJECT 3: AN EXERCISE IN YARN USAGE

You might have some yarns such as handspun, vegetable-dyed yarns, or fancy knitting yarns, which you particularly like, but only in limited quantities. Sort them and arrange them over a flat surface. If necessary, decide on a single colour to serve as a background—a neutral colour or one which tones with the others is best and should be available in whatever quantity you are likely to need. Weave a free tapestry, designing as you go. Suggested size—12 inches by 18 inches.

## PROJECT 4: INITIAL ABSTRACT

Draw a small cartoon using the initials of your name in a combination which will give you areas of differing shapes and sizes. Use yarns of the same colour, but in differing tones and textures to produce a pleasing pattern of tone and texture. Suggested size—10 inches by 15 inches.

## PROJECT 5: FUNNY FACE

With or without a cartoon, weave a face using as many techniques as possible, such as tufting for hair and eyelashes. If you lack inspiration, have a look at Else Regensteiner's book, *The Art of Weaving*, pages 6 to 13, (see Bibliography, page 63). This will give you many ideas, although it would be preferable to consult it when you have finished weaving your own design. Suggested size—12 inches by 18 inches.

## PROJECT 6: CUSHION

Wind six rounds to the inch instead of three on your frame so that you can weave two layers of tapestry, each having 6 warp ends per inch. Prepare a design for one side, and on the other, weave stripes of varying widths using the colours in your design, to make a reversible cushion cover. When you have completed the weaving you will have two layers of cloth, one for each side of the cushion.

Now, cut two weft ends and knot them with an overhand knot so that the two sides of the cushion are knotted together. Continue cutting and knotting until the two layers are joined across their width. Repeat at the other end. At each end of the cushion there will be a fringe of warp ends which should be trimmed evenly. If you use a coloured yarn for the warp, the fringe will be coloured.

Stitch together the third side (A), using a wool needle and a length of warp yarn (see Figure 40). The fourth side (B) can be finished with a zip-fastener (see Figure 40).

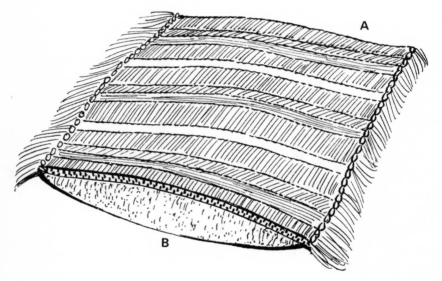

*Figure 40*

## PROJECT 7: GREEK BAG

See Project 6 for the method of weaving two layers of cloth. When both sides are woven, tie the upper and lower layers together by knotting as in Project 6. At the bottom of the bag, stitch the two selvedges together firmly with a wool needle and some warp thread. The top of the bag requires no

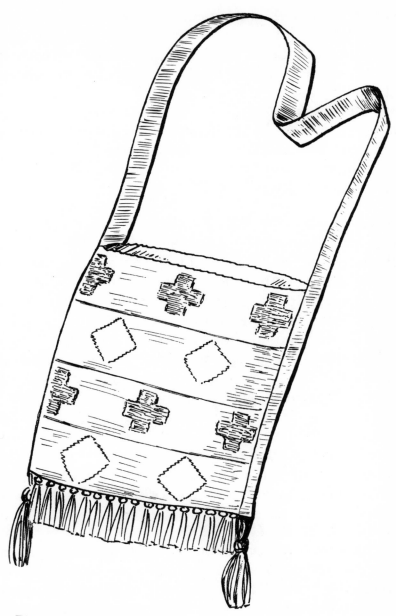

*Figure 41*

finishing. An inkle band makes a good strong handle. If attached around three sides of the bag and left free at the top for a handle of the desired length, it strengthens the sides of the bag. It can be unravelled to form a tassel at each of the bottom corners (see Figure 41).

If an inkle band is not available, try French knitting (or bobbin knitting on a cotton reel). Alternatively, make a firm twisted cord or plait with the colours you have used in the weaving.

## PROJECT 8: AN EXERCISE IN TEXTURE

Collect a number of yarns all of the same colour, such as off-white. You could use 2-ply carpet yarn as your main yarn, and as many fancy yarns as possible, including some handspun yarns. *Your Handspinning* by Elsie Davenport (see Bibliography, page 63) has many suggestions for spinning fancy yarns. Some of these will look best if, instead of being woven in, they are used for loops or tufts on the surface of the work. Many commercial yarns, such as Paton's Sea Urchin, are marketed for only a season or two, and then sold at reduced prices, as left-overs.

Use all the surface interest techniques previously described, namely rya knots, Persian knots, Spanish knots, soumak, Swedish knots, loops, and beads.

## PROJECT 9: A TRIPTYCH

A larger wall hanging can be made by designing a tapestry in three (or more) sections, to be hung side by side. They can all hang from the same rod which is woven in at the top. Weft ends can be left at the selvedges and tied to make links between the three

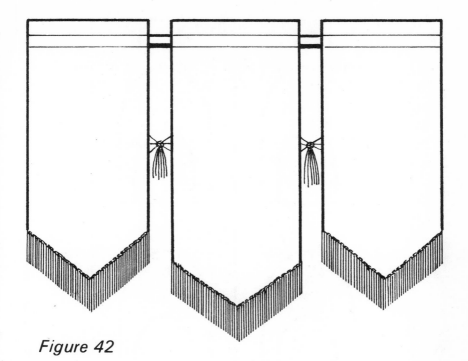

*Figure 42*

parts (see Figure 42). Alternatively, the sections could be placed much closer together. If you wish to make them longer than the 18 inches possible on your frame, use the continuous warp method (see page 14).

## PROJECT 10: A SECTIONAL RUG

From the beginning, plan your rug in sections, remembering that the units will be about 14 inches by 18 inches. Start with six units, which will make a rug 28 inches by 54 inches. When designing your rug, use squared paper with $\frac{1}{4}$- to $\frac{1}{2}$-inch squares (see Figure 43). The rug can be made with a pile, or it can be tapestry woven.

1 SQU.= $4\frac{1}{2}''$
12 X $4\frac{1}{2}$ = 54"

6 X $4\frac{1}{2}''$ = 27"
RUG = 54"X 27"

*Figure 43A*

56

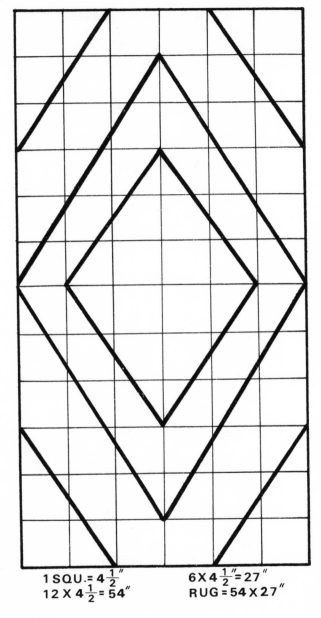

Figure 43B

You may like to make the sections identical, or you may prefer an all-over design which divides conveniently into six sections. There is no need for excessive care in matching up the sections. A slight irregularity in line where the sections meet will add to the interest of the finished rug.

Blow up the design using the simple method described on page 23, or rely on your eye if the design is not a complicated one. The eye is a surprisingly accurate instrument if used with confidence, and it becomes more efficient with use. Make an occasional check with a measuring device. Having completed the design, paint it with water colours on sketch-book paper.

## FINISHING YOUR RUG

Simply finish each end of each section of the rug as it leaves the frame with overhand knots. When six sections are completed, tie the knots at the end of one section to the knots at the end of the next. Tie them in two lots of three. Then, oversew the two strips of three-sections together down the centre on the wrong side. Use a wool needle and a double thread of warp yarn. The two ends of the yarn can be divided at the beginning and end of the stitching and tied off to finish securely.

If the knots at the ends of the rug are divided and a second row of knots made, the ends of the rug will have added protection from wear (see Figure 44). Books dealing specifically with the subject of weaving rugs, such as *Rugweaving* by Peter Collingwood (see Bibliography, page 63) give alternative methods for finishing.

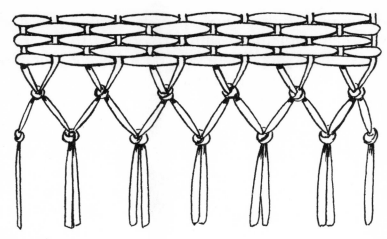

*Figure 44*

Four or five units joined on their long sides (see Figure 45), make an ideal rug, for use in front of a

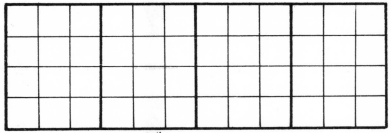

$1 \text{ SQUARE} = 4\frac{1}{2}''$
$4 \text{ SQUARES} \times 12 \text{ SQUARES} = 18'' \times 54''$

*Figure 45*

settee or lounge. Making a rug is worth considering as a winter project for the family. The frame can be picked up and worked on by any member of the family who has a little time to spare. In this case, if a harmonious colour choice is made at the start, each person can participate without spoiling the unity of the finished project. There would be a lively exchange of ideas as work progressed.

# CONDUCTING
# A WORKSHOP

A two-day workshop is an exciting introduction to tapestry weaving, and much can be accomplished in the time.

To organise a workshop there are four main things to consider:

1. A list of those who wish to participate.
2. A suitable date for the workshop.
3. A convenient place to hold the workshop.
4. A list of requirements for each member.

Plan for a four-hour day, say 10 a.m. to 3 p.m., allowing an hour for lunch, but you will probably find that enthusiasm will carry the work beyond the nominal finishing time.

Ideally, there should be a leader who has had plenty of practice in tapestry weaving. But, there may be no need for a leader if the group works directly from this book, the members comparing notes with each other as they go. If the group is operating without a leader, time can be saved in the warping of the frames if one of the group practises the warping technique beforehand.

Eight is a sensible number for a self-propelling workshop, and twelve is manageable. Fifteen is possible if there is an experienced leader, and this may even be extended to eighteen, although the leader will have less time for each individual. This can be compensated for with a follow-up session where members pass on to each other what some may have missed along the way. However, the leader will probably feel that she has not had close contact with each member, which is one of the joys of conducting a weaving workshop.

The venue depends on the amount of space available. Each weaver needs a chair and 1 square yard of table space. It is just possible for two weavers to share a card table if they sit opposite each other.

The group as a whole will need a supply of 10/12s warp cotton (about 2 ounces per person) and of basic weft yarn (about 8 ounces of 2-ply carpet yarn per person) in a good range of colours. Thrums, which can be obtained very cheaply in large quantities direct from carpet factories, are ideal. The leader will usually arrange to have these ready, or one of the group can do this.

As well, members should be given a list of the following individual requirements:
A wooden frame, approximately 24 inches by 18 inches.
A shed stick, 18 inches by 1 inch.
Notebook, pencil, and felt pen.
Dog comb, ruler, scissors or shears, and wool needle.
Tracing paper, 20 inches by 10 inches.
A projected design made up of simple shapes, about 6 inches square.
Fancy yarns including handspun yarns, and beads.

# BIBLIOGRAPHY

List A contains titles which are of practical assistance, as nearly as possible in order of usefulness for tapestry weaving. List B contains descriptive and historical books of more general interest.

## LIST A

TIDBALL, Harriet: *Contemporary Tapestry*, Shuttle Craft Guild, Michigan, (1964).

BEUTLICH, Tadek: *The Technique of Woven Tapestry*, Batsford, Lond., (1967).

TATTERSALL, Creassey Edward Cecil: *Carpet Weaving and Knotting*, Victoria and Albert Museum, Lond., (1969).

SEAGROATT, Margaret: *Rug Weaving for Beginners*, Studio Vista, Lond., (1971).

SEAGROATT, Margaret: *Coptic Weaves*, City of Liverpool Museums, (1965).

REGENSTEINER, Elsie: *The Art of Weaving*, Studio Vista, Lond.

DAVENPORT, Elsie Grace: *Your Handspinning*, Craft and Hobby Book Service, California, (1964).

Semco Booklet: *Macramé*, Semco Pty Ltd.

ATWATER, Mary Meigs: *Design and the Handweaver*, Shuttle Craft Guild, Michigan, (1961).

COLLINGWOOD, Peter: *Rugweaving*, Faber and Faber, Lond.

## LIST B

SEVENSMA: *Tapestries*, Merlin Press, Lond., (1965).

KYBALOVA, Ludmila: *Coptic Tapestries*, Paul Hamlyn, Lond., (1967).

FORMAN and WASSEF: *Tapestries from Egypt*, Paul Hamlyn, Lond., (1968).

KYBALOVA, Ludmila: *Contemporary Tapestries from Czechoslovakia*, Allan Wingate, Lond., (1963).

AMSDEN, C. A.: *Navaho Weaving*, Rio Grande Press, New Mexico, (1971).

INGERS, Gertrud: *Flemish Weaving*, Van Nostrand Reinhold, New York, (1971).

KAUFMAN, Ruth: *New American Tapestry*, Reinhold Book Corporation, (1968).

JOBE, Joseph: *The Art of Tapestry*, Thames & Hudson, Lond., (1965).

*Encyclopaedia Britannica*, Volume 21 — Tapestry.